Little Scientists, BIG Questions?

Can Animals Talk?

Tweet Tweet

Woof Woof

Ruth Owen

WINDMILL BOOKS

Published in 2020 by **Windmill Books**,
an imprint of Rosen Publishing
29 East 21st Street, New York, NY 10010

Concept development: Ruby Tuesday Books Ltd

Author: Ruth Owen
Consultant: Sally Morgan
Designer: Emma Randall
Editor: Mark J. Sachner
Production: John Lingham

Image Credits:
Alamy: 16—17; FLPA: 21 (bottom); Istock Photo: 7 (top left); Nature Picture Library: 15; Shutterstock: Cover, 1, 2—3, 4—5, 6—7, 8—9, 10—11, 12—13, 14, 18—19, 20, 22—23, 24.

Ruby Tuesday Books has made every attempt to contact the copyright holder.

Cataloging-in-Publication Data

Names: Owen, Ruth.
Title: Can animals talk? / Ruth Owen.
Description: New York : Windmill Books, 2019.
| Series: Little scientists, big questions
Identifiers: ISBN 9781725393448 (pbk.) | ISBN 9781725393462 (library bound) | ISBN 9781725393455 (6 pack)
Subjects: LCSH: Animal communication--Juvenile literature. | Animal behavior--Juvenile literature.
Classification: LCC QL751.5 O8456 2019 | DDC 591.59--dc23
Manufactured in the United States of America

CPSIA Compliance Information: Batch #BS19WM:
For Further Information contact Rosen Publishing, New York, New York at 1-800-237-9932

We LOVE to chat with our friends and family.

You're my best friend.

It's a secret.

What did you do at school today?

How are you?

She said

He said

When we meet new people, we learn all about them by talking.

Our pet dogs and cats don't use human words. But they do have ways to communicate.

A dog's bark can mean

Welcome home!

Feed me!

Someone's at the door.

I need to pee.

A cat's meow can mean

Wake up!

Feed me!

I don't like being in this crate.

Dogs and cats also use body language to communicate.

This dog is saying "play with me."

wagging tail

bottom in the air

This dog's body language says "I'm scared."

arched back

ears flat

tail between legs

This cat's tail says "I'm happy!"

This cat is afraid.

fur standing on end

ears flat to head

When you meet a friend or relative, you give them a hug.

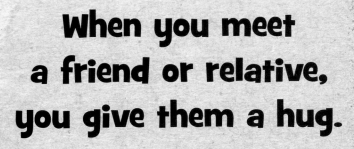

Elephants do this, too, by wrapping their trunks around each other.

A trunk hug says "I'm happy to see you!"

Elephants talk to each other in lots of ways, including low, rumbling noises.

A rumble can mean

Let's start walking.

Let's eat here.

Get ready for some **BIG** science!

Dolphins talk to each other with grunts, moans, chirps, and whistles.

Scientists use special recorders to listen to dolphins under the sea.

Scientists discovered that each dolphin has its own name.

The name is made up of squeaky whistling sounds.

Squeak Squeak Squeak Squeak Squeak

When two dolphins meet, they tell each other their whistle names.

Many animals communicate to protect each other from danger.

predator

prairie dog

Chirk Chirk Chirk

If a prairie dog spots a predator, it makes a special warning sound.

The prairie dog's family and neighbors quickly hide in their underground homes.

Prairie dogs make different "chirk-chirk" sounds for different predators.

The sound for a coyote is different from the sound for a pet dog.

coyote

hawk

pet dog

13

Umph Umph Umph Umph

Who's making this sound and what does it mean?

The sound is coming from baby crocodiles that are hatching from their eggs.

Their umph-umph-umph calls mean "Let us out!"

The crocodile eggs are buried under mud.

The mother crocodile hears her babies' cries and digs them out of their mud nest.

baby crocodile

mother crocodile

Then she carefully carries her babies to the river in her mouth.

Animals don't only use sounds for communication.

Hippopotamuses use pee and poop!

A male hippo chooses a part of a river to be his territory.

The hippo stands in the water and pees and poops.

He swings his tail from side to side, spraying poop and pee in every direction.

The poop and pee are a message to other male hippos.

"This is my territory. Keep out!"

Chameleons are lizards that communicate with their scaly skin.

A chameleon can change its skin color from green and blue . . .

. . . to orange and red!

A chameleon changes its colors to tell another chameleon it is angry or afraid.

When a male chameleon meets a female, he changes his colors.

This tells her he wants to be her mate.

Get ready for some **BIG** science!

Honeybees tell each other where to find food by dancing!

Bees gather pollen and sweet nectar from flowers.

When a honeybee finds lots of flowers, she flies back to the beehive.

beehive

Inside the hive, the bee does a waggle dance.

The bee moves in the shape of an 8.

She waggles back and forth here.

bees watching

dancing bee

The dance shows the other bees in which direction to fly.

It also tells them how far away the flowers are.

If a parrot lives with people, it may learn to say human words.

Do parrots understand what they are saying? No one knows for sure!

Hello! Nice to meet you.

Now we know that animals can talk in their own special ways.

Good work, little scientists!

23

My Science Words

communicate
To share information, news, and ideas.

predator
An animal that hunts and eats other animals.

nectar
A sugary liquid that's made by flowers.

territory
An area where an animal lives, finds food, and mates.

pollen
A dust made by flowers that is needed for making seeds.

Woof
Woof
Woof

24